Where Is It?

We Hope You Enjoy This Hidden Object Book

If You Fancy Another Challenge Then Look Up The Next Book In Our Series Over on Amazon By Typing In "Pretty Awesome Activity Books"

All Rights Reserved. No part of this book may be reproduced in any way or form or by any means whether electronic or mechanical, this means that you cannot record or photocopy any material ideas or tips that are provided in this book.

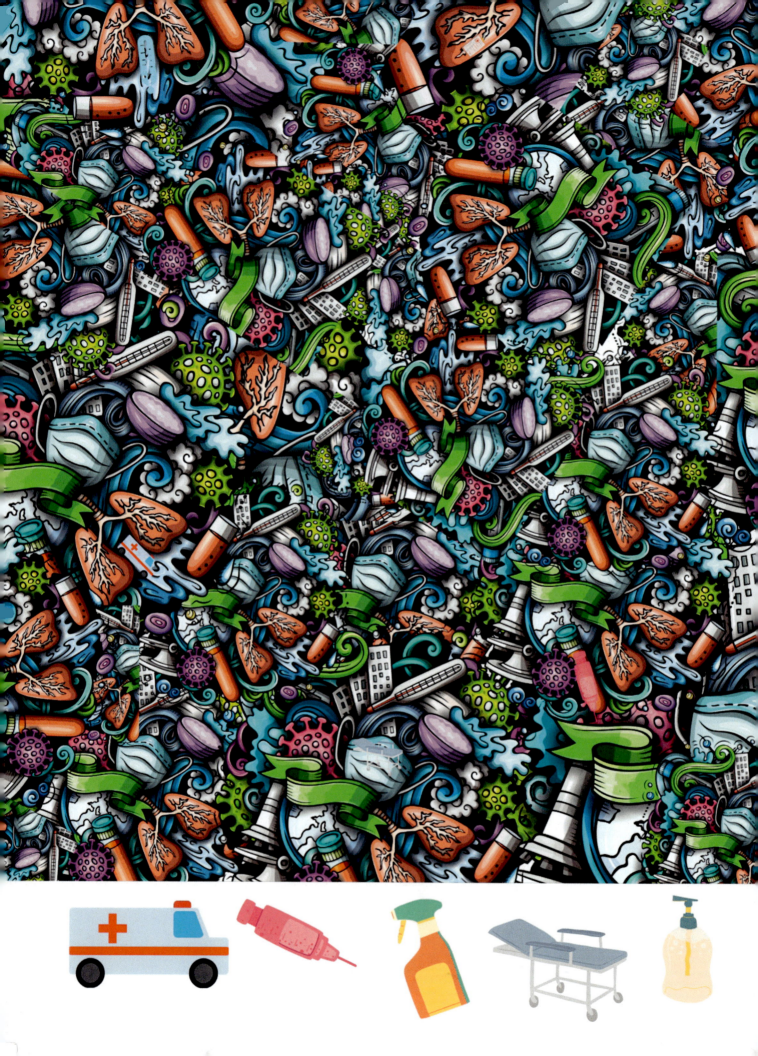

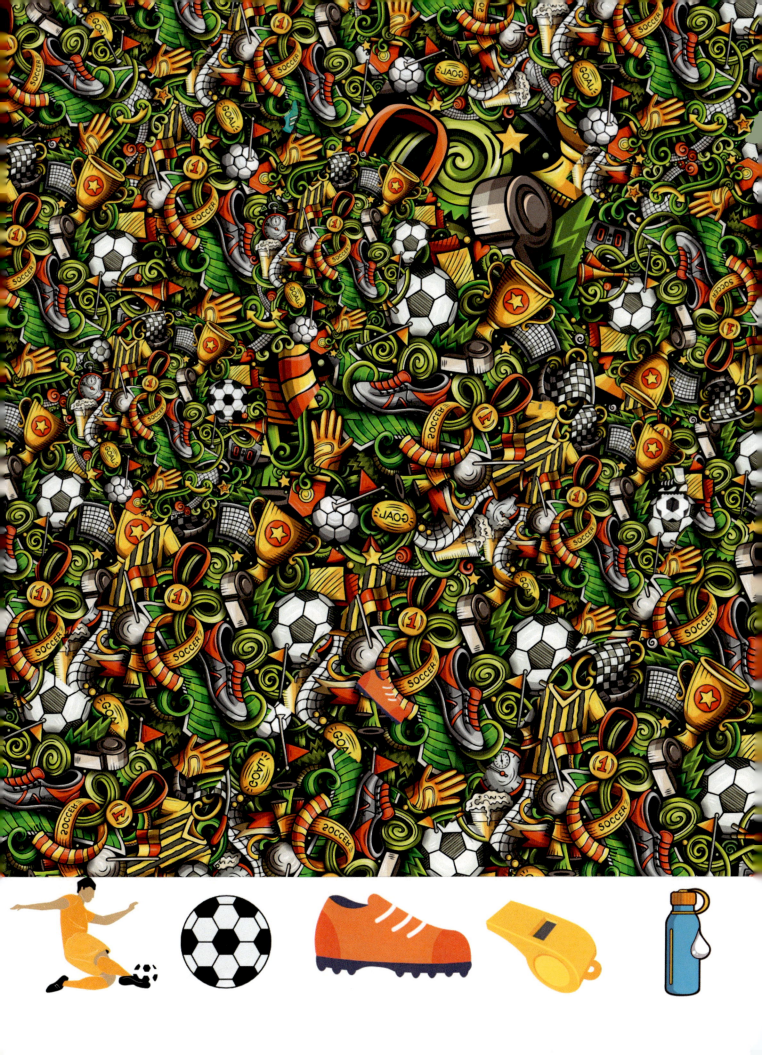

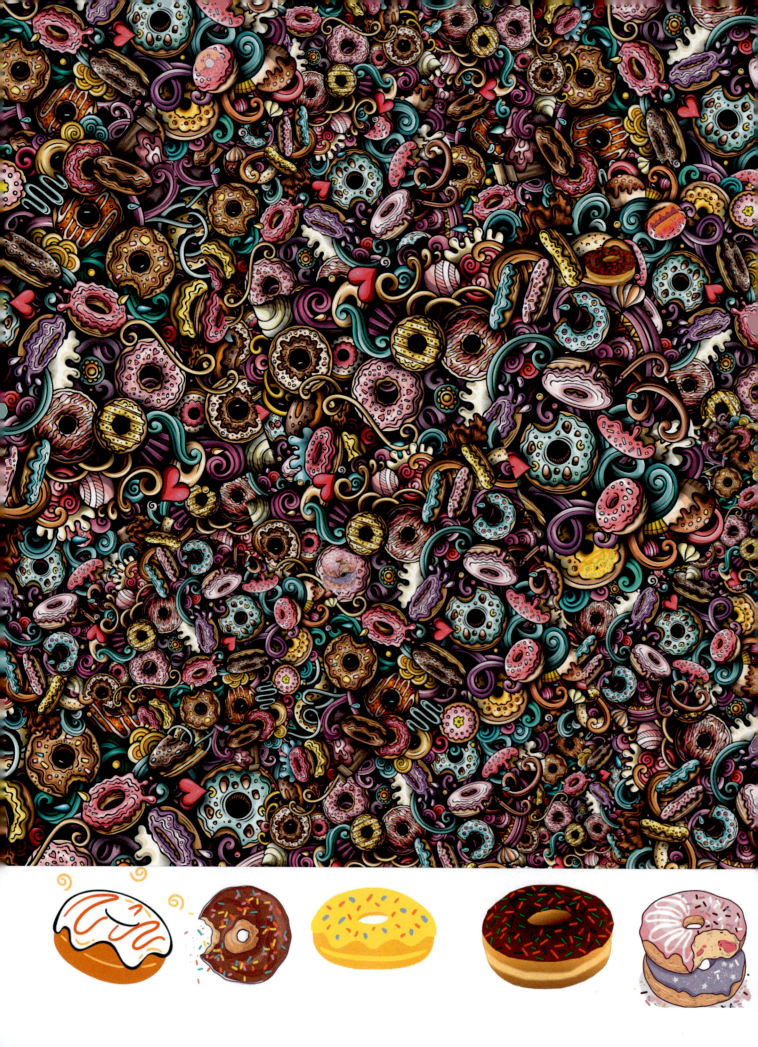

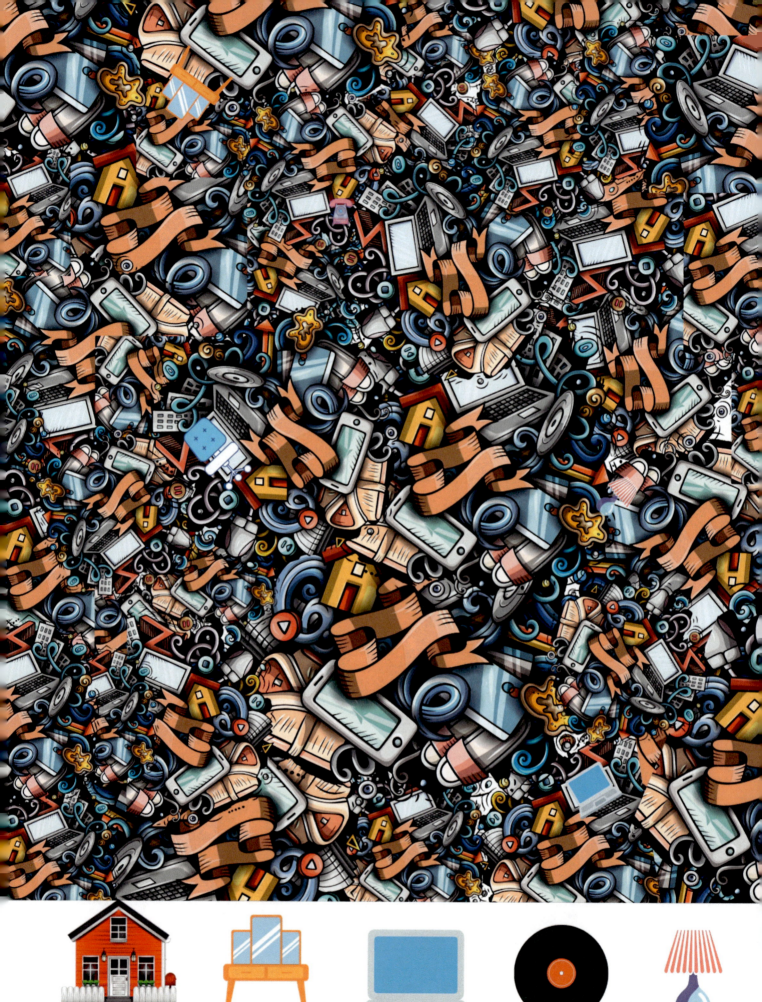

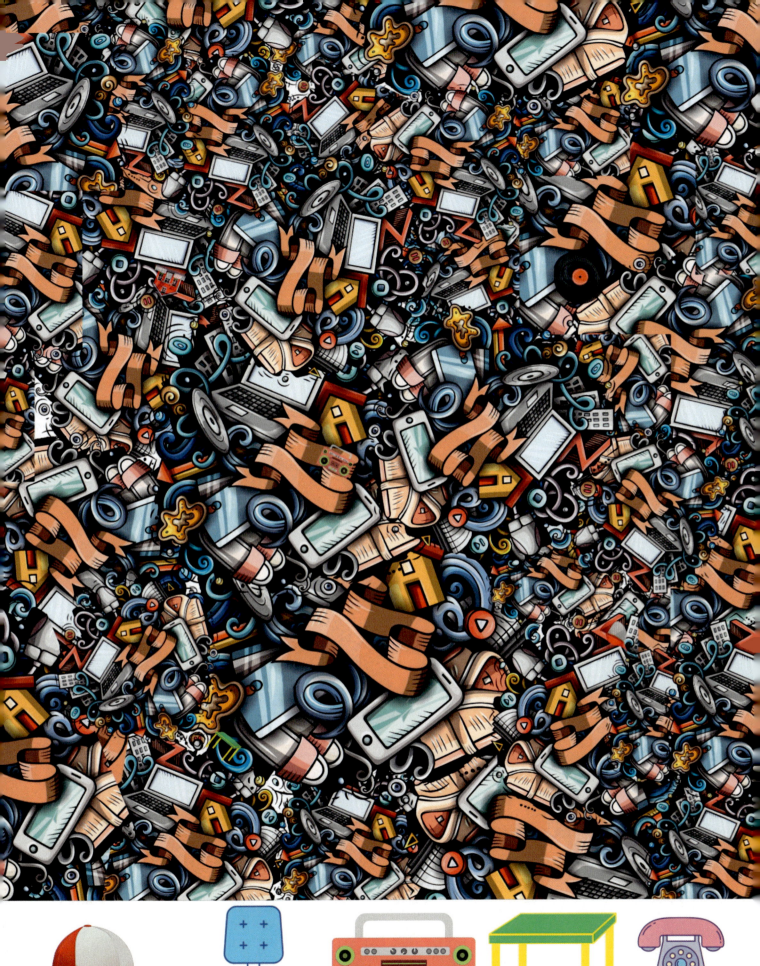

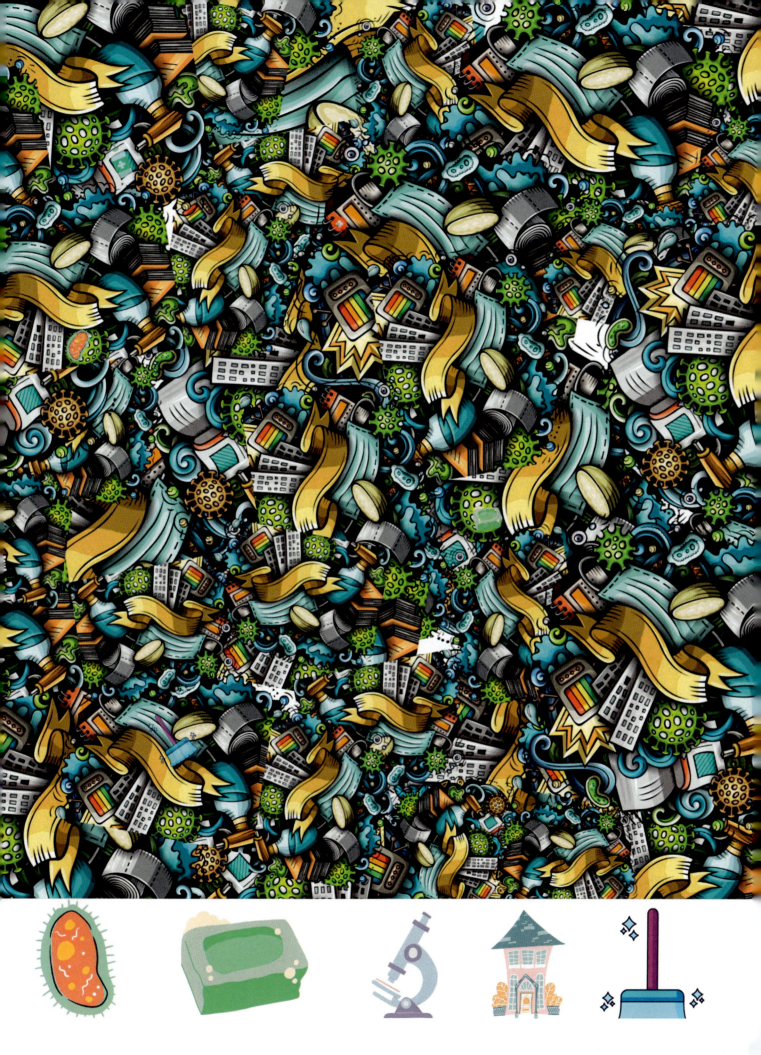

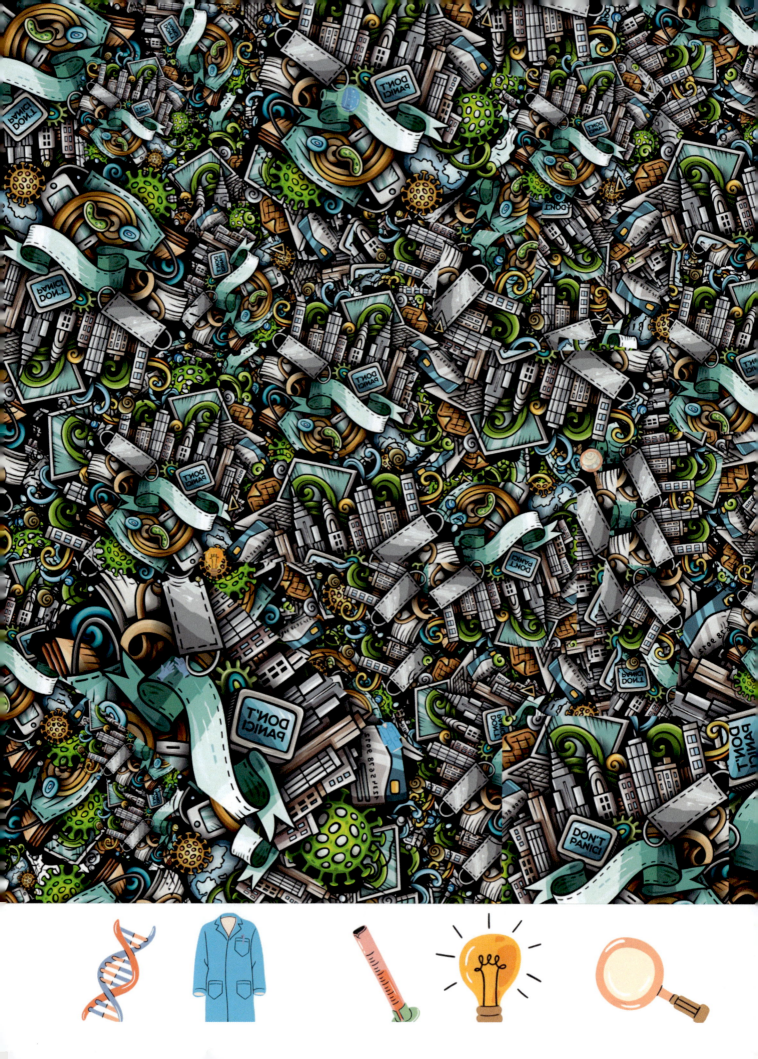

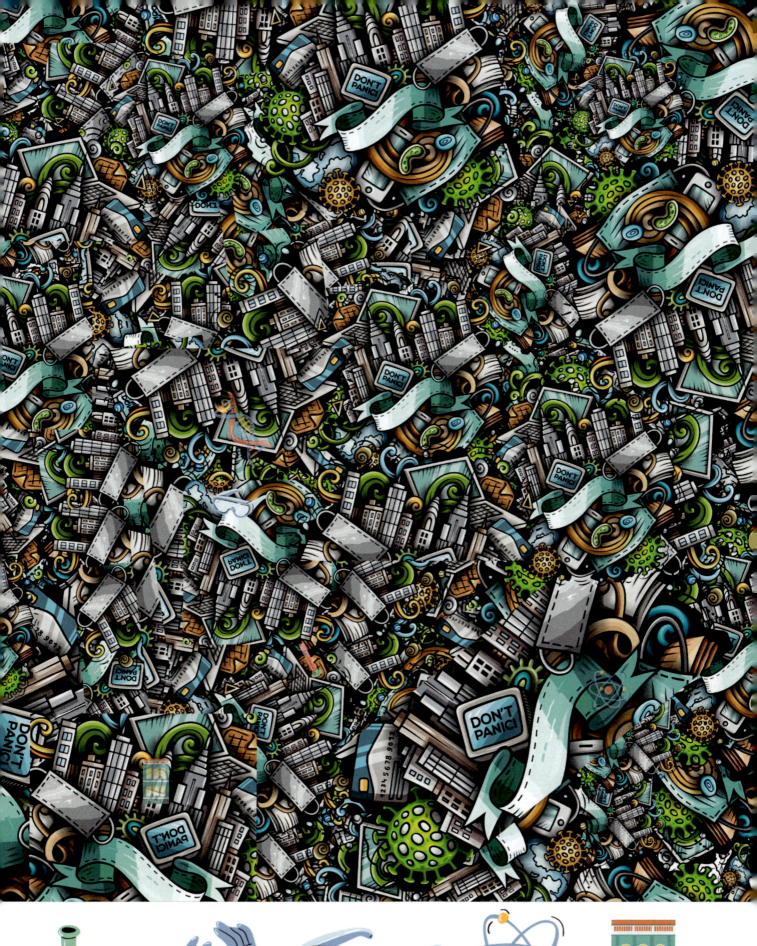
   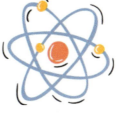 

Made in the USA
Middletown, DE
18 August 2021